REC-LEAGUE SOFTBALL

n: a sport, similar to baseball, except played
with larger, softer, slower balls
by larger, softer, slower players

Whimsical Words for Weeknight Warriors

by Dave Agans

B. MiRTHY & SONS
BOALSBURG, PA

I0324903

REC-LEAGUE SOFTBALL.
Copyright © 2025 by Dave Agans.
All rights reserved.

No part of this book may be used or reproduced in any manner whatsoever without written permission except in the case of brief quotations embodied in critical articles and reviews.

For information contact:
B. Mirthy & Sons, 400 Brush Valley Road, Boalsburg, PA 16827
www.BMirthy.com

B. Mirthy & Sons are not responsible for the content of any website or publication referenced in this book, real or fictional, except for the www.BMirthy.com website.

First edition 2025

Art by Manuel Sarmiento and Dave Agans

ISBN: 978-0-9861709-7-3 (pbk.)

Library of Congress Control Number 2025923278

*Dedicated to the Dawgs:
Celebrating 350 dog years
of softball escapades.*

Adrenaline

A bodily chemical that increases circulation and breathing rate to prepare a softball player for a crucial play. From the Greek *adrena*, to be nervous, and *Aline*, the goddess of physical misfortune.

Advance

1. To make a forward move on the basepaths, with the eventual goal of scoring.
2. To make a forward move on a spectator, with the eventual goal of scoring.

Air

Invisible gas that fills the space above the softball field. May be heavy or light, depending on temperature, humidity, and how badly hit that fly ball was.

Alive

1. Still able to win, although losing.
2. Not dead; the only requirement for playing softball.

Appeal

1. A shrewd manager, after a play is over, asking the umpire to rule on whether a baserunner has missed a base.
2. A losing manager, after a game is over, asking the players to please remember to touch all the bases next time.

Arc

1. The high curve of an effective slow pitch.
2. The sound made by a batter missing an effective high arc pitch.

Asshole

1. A fielder who questions the legality of a bat when his team is ahead 25 to 0.
2. A great place to shove an illegal bat.

At Bat

An official turn at the plate for the purpose of calculating batting average, i.e. the number of hits divided by the number of at bats. Any plate appearance counts as an at bat, except walks, hit-by-pitches, sacrifice bunts, sacrifice flies, and on base due to a fielding error when your significant other is the official scorer.

Backstop

1. A large barrier behind home plate. A regulation backstop is 28 feet wide and 1 foot shorter than the height of the average throw from the outfield.
2. A large player behind home plate.

Bag

1. Slang for a base, as in "he was tagged out 'cause he was off the bag."
2. Slang for drunk, as in "he was tagged out 'cause he was in the bag."

Balance

1. A rare quality in softball teams that allows them to hit or play the field without any weak spots in the lineup.
2. A rare quality in softball players that allows them to hit or play the field without falling over.

Balls

1. Large round objects required to play softball.
2. Small round objects required to play third base.

Base Coach

A player who stands near first or third base and, through audible or hand signals, overrules a competent baserunner's reasonable decisions.

Bat

1. A cylindrical object used to swing at a pitched ball and, occasionally, to hit one.
2. A nocturnal flying mammal with the same visual acuity as an umpire.
3. To attempt to use #1 even if blind as #2.

Batter

1. A player who is at bat, trying to hit.
2. A thick mixture of flour, eggs, and milk used to make pancakes.
3. What a manager does to a player who can't hit after eating thirty pancakes just before the game.

Beer

A miracle substance that relieves a player's anxiety about failure while simultaneously causing failure.

Blast

1. A long hit, often carrying over the fence.
2. A long post-game party, often carrying over the weekend.

Blood

A bright red bodily fluid that some baserunners wear on their legs instead of long pants.

Blooper

1. A soft pop fly, hit between the fielders, that drops in.
2. A soft pop fly, hit directly to a fielder, that is dropped.

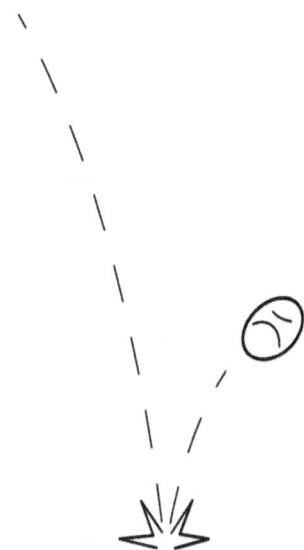

Bobble

To momentarily juggle a ball while trying to catch it. The longest bobble in recorded softball history took place on July 12, 1974 when shortstop George "Ironhands" Maladroit, playing for Apex Nitroglycerin Company, managed to keep a ball in the air for 19 seconds, while three runners scored. The ball was to have been autographed and displayed in the Softball Hall of Fame, but Maladroit was unable to get a handle on the pen.

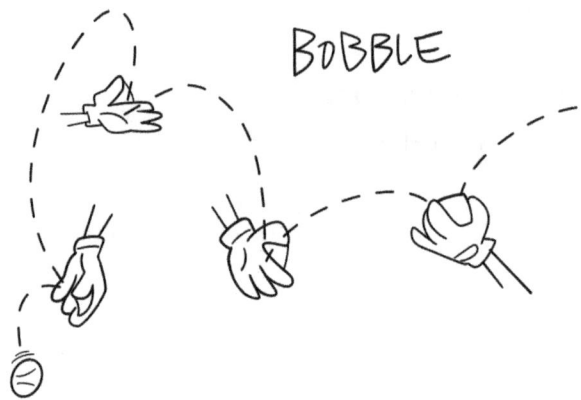

Boot

1. To kick the ball instead of fielding it cleanly.
2. An award given to a player who habitually kicks the ball instead of fielding it cleanly.

Break

1. A quick start for a baserunner, as in "She made a break for home on that sacrifice fly ball."
2. A lucky occurrence, as in "She got a break that the umpire didn't see her leave early on that sacrifice fly ball."

Bribe

Payment to an umpire in order to influence the outcome of a softball game. Absolutely not tolerated, anywhere in the world, by any softball umpire. Cash and/or beer are customary.

Bye

1. In a softball playoff, an advantage given to a first place team, allowing them to skip an early round.
2. In a softball playoff, a comment made to a last place team, indicating they will skip every round.

Can o' Corn

Along with *apple*, *pineapple*, and *piece o' cake*, a term applied to a slow moving, easy-to-catch fly ball. Statistics show, however, that it is generally more difficult to catch any of these items than a regulation softball.

Cannon

The arm of a fielder who can throw the ball with extremely high velocity. A *rifle* arm, on the other hand, means a fielder who can throw the ball with extremely high accuracy. Of course, an arm cannot be both a *cannon* and a *rifle*.

Cap

A piece of headgear designed to keep the sun out of a player's eyes. Often personalized; a fielder will adjust the strap to make it fly off dramatically during a diving catch, a manager will curl the brim to make it easier to throw to the ground in disgust, and a catcher will turn the cap around on his head to keep the umpire from drooling down his neck.

Catch

The successful grabbing of a ball by a fielder. Styles of catches include *shoestring* (at the shoetop), *basket* (both hands held out in front), and *diving* (with a horizontal leap); but no matter what the style, most catches are simultaneously *lucky*.

Catcher

A player so deemed because he spends most of his time catching pitches. Ironically, in most slow pitch leagues, this is the player least likely to be able to catch a softball.

Cemetery

A slang term for right field. Contrary to popular notion, this does not refer to the dearth of hits to right field, but rather to the liveliness of the right fielder.

Cerebral Player

Smart. A cerebral player knows the ins and outs of the game, is always aware of the situation, and cannot hit, catch, or throw.

Certified Umpire

Anyone you can find on short notice.

Chance

1. An opportunity for a fielder to make a play.
2. The overwhelming factor in determining whether a fielder will make a play.

Change Up

In fast pitch, a slow pitch. In slow pitch, a violation of fundamental physical laws.

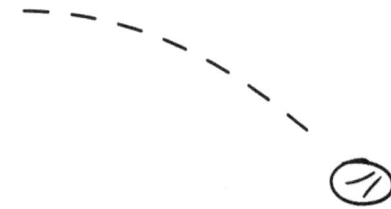

Charge

1. To move forward aggressively to field a grounder, as in, "she charged the ball since there was barely enough time to make the play."
2. To pay for on credit, as in, "she charged the ball since there was barely enough cash to buy the team bat."

Charity Hop

A ground ball that takes one high bounce, making it extremely easy for an infielder to embarrass himself by missing it.

Chatter

Trite words of encouragement shouted by fielders to give a pitcher confidence that she is the only intelligent person on the field.

Cheat

1. To move out of normal fielding position to fill a gap where a batter normally hits.
2. To add an eleventh fielder to fill a gap where a batter normally hits.

Cheers

1. Shouts of joy after a long shot that wins the game.
2. Shouts of joy before a tall shot that celebrates the win.

Choke

1. (-up): Grip the hands higher on the bat to assure a hit in a critical situation.
2. Strike out in a critical situation.
3. Grip the hands tighter around the neck of the player who struck out in a critical situation.

Clutch Hit

A hit when desperately needed. One of many softball terms of automotive origin, for example: although *tired*, even *exhausted*, the team *spark plug* will often *belt* a long *drive*, to the cheering of the *fans*.

Cock

After fielding a ground ball, to draw one's arm back and hold it there for a split second, before throwing the runner out at first.

Cocky

After fielding a ground ball, to draw one's arm back and hold it there for five seconds, before throwing the runner out at first.

Coincidence

Two things occurring in the same place at the same time. For example: a fielder is running sideways and the ball is moving outward and downward; when the mitt and the ball arrive at the same place simultaneously, it is a coincidence.

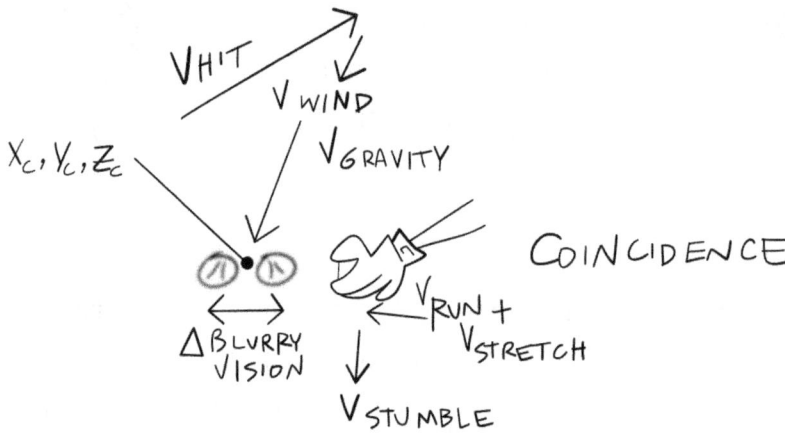

Collide

When two players call "I got it" and don't hear each other, they often collide, dropping the ball. From Latin *co* (both) and *lied* (said they would catch it).

Commit

To make an irreversible move. A runner *commits* when, caught halfway between first and second, he makes his final dash for second base; the fielder *commits* an error by throwing to first.

Conference

A conversation on the mound, among the pitcher, catcher, and sometimes infielders, to discuss the situation, the batter, or where to go for beers after the game.

Conservative

Unwilling to take risks. Conservative fielders back up to avoid letting hits through, conservative runners hold up if they're not sure they can make it to the next base, and conservative managers collect the team fee before letting a player play.

Contact

A measure of the solidity with which a batter has struck the ball. When a batter says "I made good contact" it means the ball was struck directly, in the center of the bat, traveled straight at high speed, and was caught.

Contest

1. A softball game.
2. To argue a call. To some managers, also a game.

Costly Error

A mistake with major bad consequences, such as dropping a fly ball with two out in the bottom of the ninth, bases loaded, and a one run lead, or adding a tip to the post-game restaurant bill even though the waiter already added it automatically for such a large crowd.

Cover the Bag

To stand near a base, ready to tag a runner who tries to reach it. A good infielder will literally cover the bag, so that the runner must literally run through the fielder to reach it. A good runner, however, will do so, literally covering the bag with teeth and blood.

Crack

Crank

1. To hit the ball very hard and very far, often over the fence.
2. The crotchety old man whose picture window is just beyond the fence.

Curve

A ball that is thrown with enormous spin, making it change direction dramatically in mid-flight, and making its path extremely difficult to predict. Usually thrown by the third baseman on a routine play to first.

Cut

A play wherein an infielder intercepts a throw from the outfield to the plate, that will not reach home in time to catch the runner, in order make a throw to another base, that will not reach the base in time to catch the other runner.

Dally

To advance to the next base on a down-the-line double.

Dark

A signal to begin the sixth inning. Not to be confused with *dawn*, the signal to end the post-game party.

Dead

1. Sure to be thrown out, as in, "the runner was dead since the third base coach waved her home while the shortstop had the ball."
2. Lifeless, as in, "the third base coach was dead since the manager saw him wave the runner home while the shortstop had the ball."

Defense

De ting dat home runs go over.

Diamond

Dive

1. A low, horizontal jump for a batted ball.
2. A low, disreputable joint for a post-game beer.

Double Header

Back-to-back games added to the loss column.

Double Play

A fielding play where two outs are made in quick succession.

Double Take

The manager's reaction to a double play.

Ducks on the Pond

The bases are loaded with runners, ready for a grand slam home run. This term originated from the runners' resemblance to ducks, resulting from the "bills" on their caps, and the way they "run."

Elimination

Occurs after one loss in a single elimination tournament, after two losses in a double elimination tournament, and after drinking three beers and going behind the bushes in any tournament.

Equipment

Items required to play softball, including bats, balls, gloves, spikes, bases, helmets, masks, coolers, beer, and ice. Notably missing from this list are skill, responsibility, uniforms, cash for team fees, and car keys.

Error

The outcome of an attempt to catch or throw.

Exercise

A conditioning activity recommended for softball but not provided by it.

Eyes

When a ground ball slithers its way through the infield, just out of reach of several players, it is said that the ball *had eyes*. Usually, however, it's just that the fielders *didn't*.

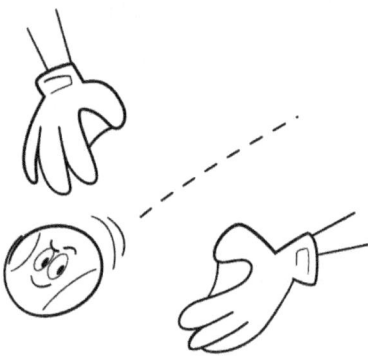

Fair Ball

Round, no broken stitches, was only left in the rain once or twice.

Fan

1. To strike out.
2. A person who enjoys watching your softball games, even if you strike out.

Fast Pitch

A style of softball in which the pitches are very rapid and hard to hit. Because of the speed of the ball and the small size of the infield, fast pitch softball has even more intensity than baseball. The alternative is slow pitch softball, in which the pitches are quite slow and easy to hit, giving the game an intensity somewhere between golf and croquet.

Fielder's Choice

The scoring of a play where the batter could have been thrown out at first, except that the fielder chose to throw the ball somewhere else, such as into the bleachers behind third base.

Flat

1. The vertical path of an easy-to-hit slow pitch.
2. The body position of a pitcher who has just thrown a flat pitch.

Fly Ball

A batted ball that travels far and high in the air until being missed by an outfielder.

Force Out

To get the ball to a base to which a runner must run. Similar terms include: *tag out*, to touch the ball to an off-base player; *toss out*, to eject a drunk, argumentative player; and *pass out*, to become a drunk, non-argumentative player.

Foul Ball

A ball that has been stored in the trunk of your car under the lucky socks you've worn without washing for 87 consecutive games.

Foul Tip

Wear those lucky socks when you go out after the game; your date will be impressed that you're such a jock.

Full Count

Three balls, two strikes, ten fielders, fifteen paid team fees, six beers.

Fuller Count (for kids)

Fundamentals

Basic softball know-how. Some of the fundamentals:
   Keep your eye on the ball.
   Get your glove down on grounders.
   Hold the bat by the narrow end.

Gamble

To attempt a daring catch of a sinking line drive rather than hang back and make the conservative one-hop play. The reward is an out instead of a hit, but the risk is a ball that goes through for extra bases. Most players take the gamble since, considering the likelihood of making even a conservative catch, they have nothing to lose.

Gap

The area between fielders where a batted ball is likely to go past them. Also known as the *seams*, *alleys*, or *holes*. On some slow teams, known as the *boulevards* or the *grand canyons*.

Ground Ball

A batted ball that bounces along the ground until being missed by an infielder.

Guard the Line

To play just a step from the first or third base line, in order to prevent "down the line" doubles, instead forcing the batter to hit "through the gap" doubles.

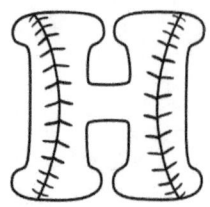

Halfway

The point between two bases where runners go on a fly ball, so that no matter whether it is caught or missed they will be barely unable to make it to the correct base.

Heave

1. Toss the ball with great physical exertion.
2. Breathe heavily after great physical exertion.
2. Toss cookies after great physical exertion.

Hit

1. A batted ball that allows the batter to reach first safely.
2. A popular thing; e.g., reaching first safely.

Hit for the Cycle

To hit a single, a double, a triple, and a homer in the same game. Not to be confused with *hit for the haiku*, which is:

  To hit or strike out
  Summer is not judgmental
  Cool green grass remains.

Homer

A hit in which the batter runs all the way around the four bases. Named for the Greek writer Homer, whose tale of an arduous ten-year adventure in the Odyssey seems quick and easy compared to an out-of-shape slugger huffing and puffing around the basepaths.

Hot Corner

A nickname for third base, due to the large number of blistering grounders and searing line drives that are hit there. Third basemen, as a result, must have lightning reflexes and nerves of steel. By contrast, first base, which has almost no such demanding action, is sometimes referred to as the *cool corner*, the *lazy corner*, and the *home for aging infielders*.

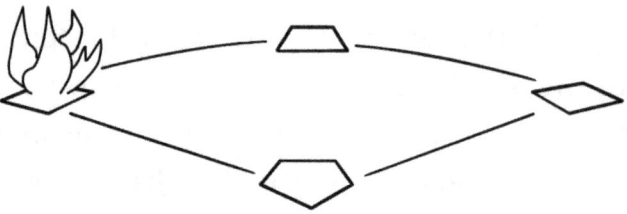

Hustle

To move about quickly and with great energy, convincing players to sign up for yet another expensive weekend tournament.

Infield Fly Rule

A rule that states that when there are none or one out, runners in forced position, and the batter hits a pop fly to the infield, the umpire shall call in a loud voice "infield fly, batter is out!" This phrase is meaningless to all players and most umpires.

Injury

A physical problem that causes softball play to be painful. However, this is indistinguishable from the play of a healthy softball player.

Inside Pitch

A pitch that crosses the plate close to the batter. A pitch away from the batter is called an *outside pitch*. A fast inside pitch to the head is called an *upside pitch*.

Insurance Runs

Runs scored by a team that is already leading, as "insurance" against the other team scoring later in the game. As with real insurance, clumsy, error-prone teams require lots of insurance. Many teams are uninsurable.

Interference

An infraction committed by a runner who purposefully or accidentally prevents the fielders from blowing the play themselves.

In the Black

1. A slow pitch that hits the black border of the plate; ideal, but difficult to achieve.
2. A team fund with a positive balance; ideal, but difficult to achieve.

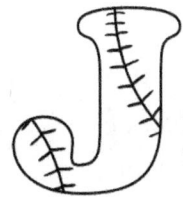

Jam

A sticky situation for a pitcher, with runners on base and not many outs. When pitchers repeatedly get into jams, they're toast.

Judgment Call

A ruling that depends on the umpire's opinion about what happened, rather than on an interpretation of the rules. For example: the umpire thinks a runner left early on a sacrifice fly. The rule against this is clear, and whether the runner actually left early is not open to discussion. The umpire will observe the size of the runner's manager and the length of his recent prison term for second degree assault, and make the judgment call that the runner did not leave early.

Jump

A quick start. A fielder anticipates which way a ball will be hit, and at the moment the ball leaves the bat, "jumps" in the opposite direction.

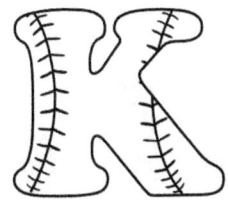

K

The scoring symbol for striKeout. Other commonly used symbols are BB (Base on Balls), FC (Fielder's Choice), and SAC (Sacrifice). Less commonly used symbols are SOP (Stepped On Plate), TB (Threw Bat), and THDFBL (Tripped Halfway Down First Base Line).

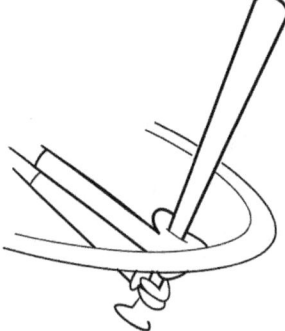

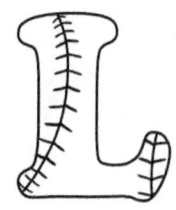

Lazy

Said of a fly ball that is softly hit, not too short or too deep, and high enough to give the fielder time to get under it, if he wasn't so lazy.

Lead

1. (-off): What the first batter in an inning is.
2. (-off first): What a runner at first base takes.
3. (-out): Once the ball is hit, what the batter and the runner have to get the.

Lefty
A player who cannot loan or borrow a mitt.

Leg It Out
To hustle to first base in order to beat the throw. An archaic term, no longer used once a softball player reaches drinking age.

Line
1. Long stripe of chalky powder that defines the edge of the playing field in a softball game.
2. Short stripe of chalky powder that puts an edge on the playing experience for participants in the annual New York vs. Los Angeles celebrity softball game.

Line Drive
A batted ball that travels rapidly and directly before being missed by the short fielder.

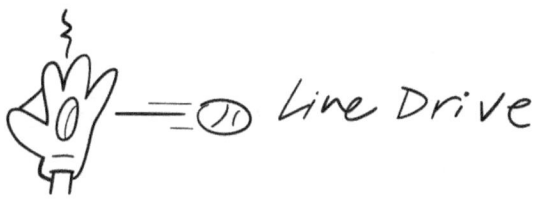

Lineup

1.

2.

Look at a Pitch

Avoid swinging at the first pitch, to get into the rhythm of the pitcher and try to get ahead in the count. Batters who do this should look closely, as the first pitch will be the only hittable one they get.

Look the Runner Back

When a player fields a ground ball, and there are runners on base who are not forced, the fielder will often "look the runners back" before throwing to first, so that if any of them decided to run, they would be caught off base and tagged out. Other phrases for this technique are *checking the runner* and *holding the runner*. With some fast runners, stronger measures are required, such as *threatening the runner, tying the runner's shoelaces together,* or *mining the basepath*.

Makeup Game

1. Ad hoc game that replaces one that was postponed due to weather.
2. Annual San Francisco vs. Provincetown drag softball championship.

Manager

The leader of a softball team. Nicknames include *chief, coach, captain, stupid jerk,* and *pompous asshole.*

Meat of the Bat

The wide part of the bat; the best place to hit the ball. Other parts are the *tip of the bat* (a bad place to hit the ball); the *label of the bat* (a good place to break the bat); the *handle of the bat* (a good place to break your fingers); and the *point of the bat* (to hit the ball).

Meatball

A slow, easy-to-hit pitch. Also *melon*. While some experts attribute the melon reference to the apparent size of the ball as it approaches the batter, it is exceeding rare for a meatball to even reach, much less exceed, the size of a softball. Recent research has determined that both of these terms derive from a culinary, rather than physical, phenomenon: batters have been observed with their mouths watering as the pitch approaches.

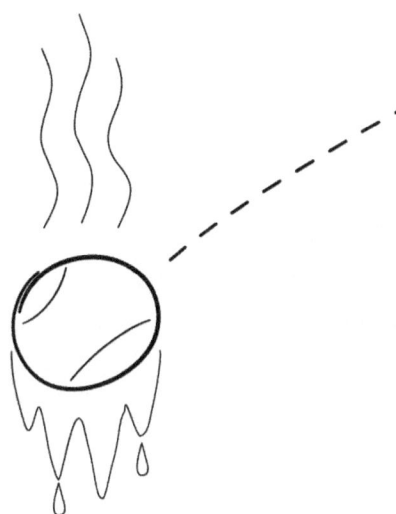

Mitt

A loosely laced, poorly fitting, dry and slippery device used to protect a fielder's hand from blame for missed catches.

Mound

A raised area where the *rubber*, a marker for where the pitcher stands, is mounted. Like many softball terms, *"mound"* represents the ideal, but is typically just a bare spot in the grass. Likewise, the *"rubber"* is just a line in the dirt, and the *"pitcher"* is just somebody too old or slow to play any other position.

Muff

To commit a fielding error. Other terms include *misplay, mishandle, misjudge, bobble, drop, blow, screw up, boot, miss,* and *botch*. In fact, similarly to the celebrated Eskimo vocabulary of 27 words for snow, there are more words for fielding error than any other concept in the softball lexicon.

Must Win

Will Lose.

Nail

One of many fastener terms used in softball, meaning to make a sharp *peg* to throw out a *bolting* runner. If not *screwed* up, it can be a *riveting* play in a high *stakes* game.

Neet's Foot Oil

A substance that is regularly applied to every player's glove, to keep it soft and flexible, in the manager's dreams. Other animal podiatry products used on softball gloves include *rabbit's foot oil*, to induce lucky catches; *camel's foot oil*, to drink up the disgusting sweat left inside when someone borrows your glove; and *skunk's foot oil*, to discourage people from borrowing your glove in the first place.

Night Game

A game wherein it is during the first inning, rather than the seventh, that the children at home wonder why only one parent is tucking them in again.

On Deck

Next in line to bat. The player after the on deck batter is referred to as *in the hole*. The subsequent batters are usually *on the bench*, except for the guy who's had four beers, who is *behind the bushes*.

One Pitch League

A boring softball variation characterized by muscular players hitting nothing but home runs or fly outs. For teams who joined thinking they would have fun, also a *One Season League*.

Opponent

The enemy in a softball game. In various contexts may be a team, a player, an umpire, or a coach, but typically, the ball.

Orthodox

Conventional; rigid. Often said of a team that always plays the percentages, never takes risks, and refuses to play on Saturday.

Out

1. A batted ball that does not allow the batter to reach first safely.
2. Unpopular; e.g., not reaching first safely.

Outfielder

A player who plays beyond the infield. There are three outfield positions: *Left Fielder, Center Fielder* and *Right Fielder*. In slow pitch, a fourth is added, the *Short Fielder*, who can also play as the *Left Center Fielder*. Other variations include the *Way Out in Left Fielder*, the *Outstanding in His Fielder*, and, in backyard games, the *Leach Fielder*.

Overrun a Base

Give 110% on the basepaths.

Paunch

Abdominal area developed by softball players through high repetitions of elbow bending exercises.

Pine Tar Rag

A lively 1890s tune by Scott Joplin in tribute to the newly-invented game of softball.

Pitcher

The player who delivers pitches to the batter. Throwing an average of five pitches to each batter can be tiring, and as a result, many pitchers need relief in mid-game. See *Relief Pitcher*.

Pizza

The traditional post-game meal, for three reasons: First, hearty pizza is especially appetizing to muddy, sweaty players after a tough game. Second, messy pizza is no problem to players who are already muddy and sweaty. Third, pizza parlors are the only restaurants that will allow muddy, sweaty players past the front door.

Plant

1. To dig in, as in "the catcher planted himself in front of the plate to stop the runner from scoring."
2. To cause the death and burial of, as in, "the runner planted the catcher who tried to stop her from scoring."

Platoon

To alternate a group or pair of players in successive innings or games. From the Latin *plao* (to play) and *toena* (inconsistently).

Plug

When a small chunk of fine, aromatic chewing tobacco, such as Skoal™, is inserted into a softball player's cheek and mentioned in a softball dictionary, it is called a plug.

Pop-Up

A ball hit straight up. In keeping with Newton's third law of motion, the equal and opposite reaction is a bat thrown straight down.

Puddle

The smooth part of the infield.

Put Him On

1. Intentionally walk a power hitter on four outside pitches rather than risk a long hit.
2. Tell your manager you threw those four outside pitches intentionally.

Quadruple

An unused term for a four-base hit. Though *quadruple* is the natural next term in the progression of *single, double,* and *triple,* it has been replaced by *home run,* much to the chagrin of softball dictionary writers who can't think of any softball-related word that begins with Q.

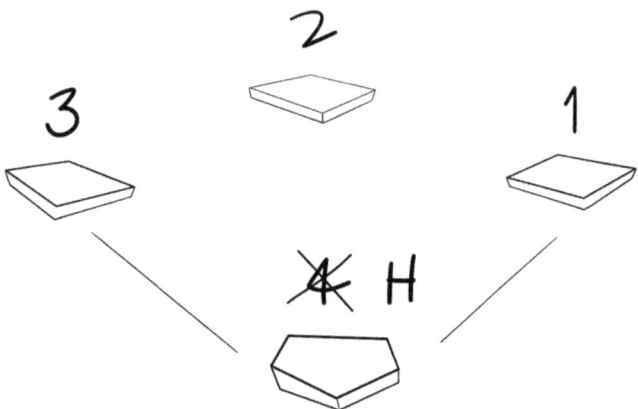

Raffle

1. A common fund-raising mechanism for softball leagues where tickets are sold by players and a prize is awarded to the holder of the winning ticket.
2. A firearm that is a common prize in southern softball leagues.

Rain

One of many atmospheric conditions that may be present at softball games. Other conditions include cold, wind, lightning, sweltering heat, humidity, black flies, mosquitoes, black flies *and* mosquitoes, cold *and* rain *and* wind *and* lightning, and sweltering heat *and* humidity *and* black flies *and* mosquitoes.

Rally Caps

The ritual practice of turning all caps brim-backward when the team needs a late-game scoring rally to come from way behind. Has a twofold effect: inspires the team to keep the rally going, and makes the team look like the losers they will soon become. Less successful garments that have been attempted for this purpose include rally shirts, rally shoes, and rally underwear.

Rap

The dude is hot
Hits a strong swat
A long shot to the parking lot
Or just a slap
Through the gap
You say as you dap him up
"Nice rap."

RBI

Runs Batted In; an indicator of batting effectiveness. A more accurate measure of batting performance, however, is IBP (Ideal Batting Performance), which is the sum of RBI and RIWHBIITRWSDS (Runs I Would Have Batted In If The Runner Wasn't So Damned Slow).

Red Dot

Also *blue dot*, *gold dot*, and *gray dot*; a marking on the ball indicating how far it will fly. Red dot balls fly the furthest and thus are not recommended for softball games in crowded suburban areas. Other dots and their meanings include *green dot*, which won't fly into fragile, endangered ecosystems; *yellow dot*, which is afraid to fly anywhere; and *brown dot*, which doesn't fly worth shit.

Reflex

An instantaneous surge of motion as a fielder reacts to a hit ball.

Reflux

An instantaneous surge of stomach acid as a manager reacts to fielders with no reflexes.

Relief Pitcher

A container of cold beer to refresh a tired player.

Ringer

A talented player who is not a member of a team but is secretly brought in to help win crucial games. Ringers are easy to spot: look for the guy with arms as big as the other players' thighs, introducing himself to those players before the game.

Rip

Roster

A list of people who would show up for games if they didn't have something more important going on that night.

'Round the Horn

A stylish, good-luck procedure performed at the start of each inning in which the catcher throws the ball to the shortstop, who flips it to the second baseman, who throws it to the third baseman, who is busy ducking the outfield warm-up ball (just thrown toward the third base bench) and misses it, then apologizes to the mother of the toddler hit by the ball, who angrily grabs it and fires it to the pitcher.

Rout

A game in which your team gets clobbered.

Routine

Typical. Often used to describe a play or game. Routine is derived from *rout*, to get clobbered.

Run

The basic unit of scoring in softball, tallied when a player crosses home plate. Appropriately, a run requires running. This is why some teams don't get many.

Rundown

1. A play where a runner is trapped between two bases, running back and forth until either tagged out or safely on base.
2. How a runner feels after such a play.

Rec-League Softball

Schedule

A list of evenings when softball games will be rained out.

Seeing-Eye Single

A base hit that passes through a tight gap in the infield, chased by the umpire's dog.

Serious League

As distinguished from ordinary, play-for-fun leagues, some leagues' intent is to play softball with great intensity, endurance, and athletic skill. Right. Get serious.

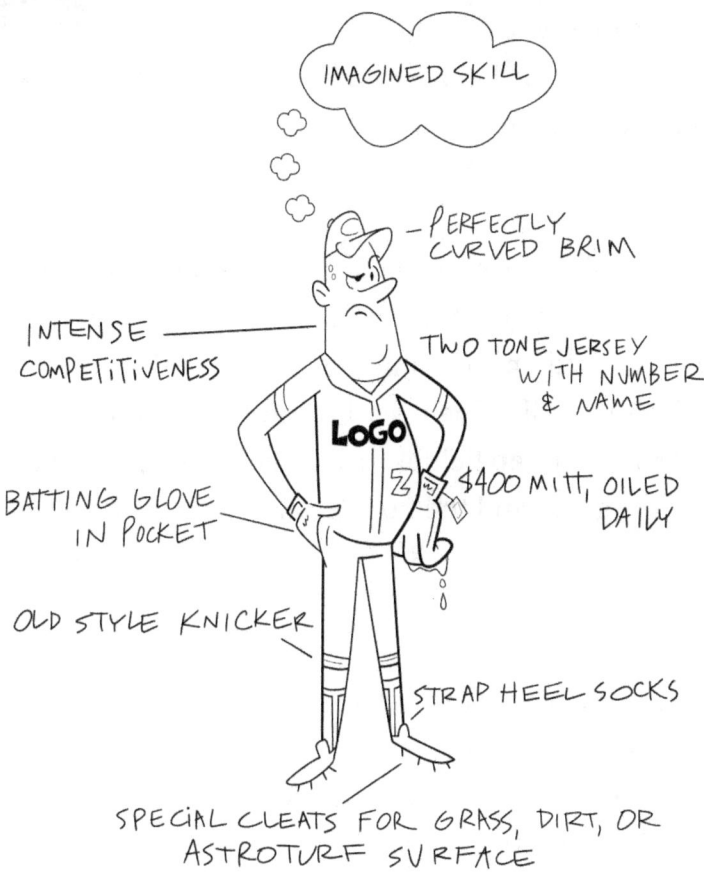

Shag

To field balls hit during batting practice. There are several possible Olde English origins for this term, including *sharg*, one who retrieves errant sheep; *shago*, free laborer; and *shagge*, stupid but energetic puppy dog.

Shallow

Fielders can play shallow or deep. Shallow fielders are usually used in the bottom of the last when the winning run is on third; they play close to the infield, focused on stopping the game-winning hit, and neglecting the long ball, which would result in a game-winning sacrifice fly anyway. Deep fielders are usually lost in thought about the emptiness of the game and the hopelessness of ever winning anything of value.

Shift

1. A defensive tactic where the fielders all move to one side, to stop a good hitter who cannot hit the other way.
2. A change in tactics, such as going back to a straight-away defense when a good hitter shows she *can* hit the other way.

Shutout

1. When one team fails to score because the defense is perfect.
2. When both teams fail to score because the fence is locked.

Sign

A hand signal performed by a third base coach. Typical signs and their meanings include: touching the brim of the hat (*steal*), wiping the left shoulder (*hit and run*), and wiping the chin (*damn, that's good kielbasa*).

Sinking Liner

A hard-hit ball that clears the infield but before reaching the outfield strikes an iceberg and slips below the waves with great loss of life, several movies and a Broadway musical.

Slide

1. To approach a base without standing.
2. To approach the basement of the standings.

Slugging Average

A calculation of a player's long shots, where a single is worth one, a double is worth two, etc., divided by the number of times he steps up to the bar.

Smoke

1. A pitch so fast that the batter has trouble seeing the ball.
2. Cigarette combustion product so thick that the shortstop has trouble seeing the ball.

Snow Cone

A catch in which the ball protrudes from the web of the glove so as to resemble the popular frozen treat. Ironically, a very uncool catch.

Spirit

1. Enthusiasm that can contribute to a team's success.
2. Alcoholic beverage that can contribute to a team's enthusiasm.

Split

Sometimes a team wins the opening game of a doubleheader, but then loses the second because their star shortstop split for a hot date after the first game.

Spoiler

1. A rotten team that, in the last game of the season, beats a contending team, ruining the contenders' chances of making the league playoffs.
2. A rotten sandwich that, after the last game of the season, is left in the cooler, ruining the cooler's chances of being used again.

Sponsor

A business that chooses to put its name on softball jerseys rather than billboards, since softball jerseys are much cheaper and almost as large.

Sprain

A twisting injury, usually to the ankle, where the tissue is severely damaged. The ankle is susceptible to other similar injuries: a *strain* is usually caused by stretching the ankle; a *scrape* is caused by sliding into base; a *break* is caused by having your foot in the way when someone slides into base; and an *aluminumb* is caused by tapping the mud off your cleats with a bat and hitting your ankle instead.

Squibler

A rapidly spinning ground ball that bounces erratically. A variation is *squabler*, which is a rapidly spinning ground ball that bounces erratically off a baby pigeon.

Stab

1. A lunging catch that robs the batter of a sure hit.
2. A lunging retaliation method contemplated by batters who've been robbed of a sure hit.

Stance

The body position of a batter. An *open stance* means the batter is facing toward the pitcher. A *closed stance* means the batter is facing away from the pitcher. A *circumstance* is that the batter can't hit no matter which way he faces.

Stand Up

A phrase spoken by a third base coach meaning "stop, but no need to slide" as the runner approaches third. Other phrases include *hit it*, meaning "slide;" *take a turn*, meaning "look to see if you can go home;" and *back*, meaning "you idiot, the third baseman has the ball already."

Stick

A nickname for the bat. Other popular nicknames include *club*, *lumber*, and *waste of eighty-nine dollars*.

Stretch

To extend, as in "I stretched the single into a double by running aggressively," or "He stretched the truth about that single the outfielder bobbled."

Stroke

1. A smooth, clean hit.
2. A manager's medical emergency caused by watching their pitcher give up lots of smooth, clean hits.

Subs

Players who replace the starting team when the puddles on the field get too deep.

Swat

1. To hit a homer.
2. To hit a mosquito, especially if the mosquito's name is Homer.

Switch-Hitter

A batter who is equally ineffective from both sides of the plate.

Target

The catcher's mitt held out for the pitcher to aim at. This has been proven to help pitchers get the ball over the plate, though it is not always successful. In 1987, playing against power-hitting Flo's Tavern, Crystal Drycleaning catcher Flash McMugg attempted to correct his pitcher's aim once and for all by secretly substituting an iron-core softball into play, and mounting a powerful electromagnet in his glove that could pull the ball to it with 400 pounds of force. Unfortunately, on the first pitch, McMugg suffered a concussion off the left field wall.

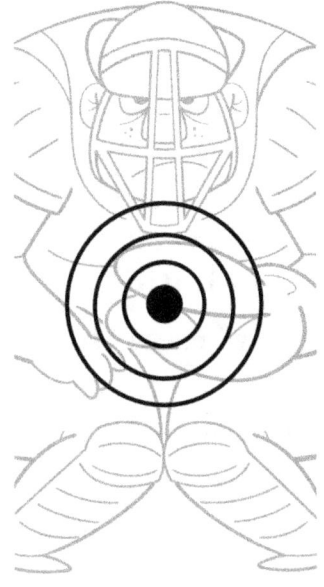

Tater

A long shot, resulting in a home run. For most players, a longshot. Thought to originate from the slang for potato, but other possible sources are *tata* (goodbye), *trotter* (jog around the bases), and *torture* (itch for days from the poison ivy picked up while retrieving the ball from the meadow beyond the fence).

Team Photo

A blurry image of some of the players on a cloudy day.

Ten Run Rule

A rule that allows a team losing by a large margin to declare an early end to the game. Supported by tiring umpires and humiliated teams. Opposed by softball fanatics and stat-obsessed batters who are 7 for 7 with 4 homers going into the fifth inning.

Texas Leaguer

A batted ball that travels weakly in the air before being missed by both an infielder and an outfielder.

Tie Goes to the Runner

A statement indicating that the speaker is on the batting team. Other such identifying phrases are *"she missed the tag,"* *"he trapped it,"* and the ever popular, *"that was way outside!"* Antonyms: *"he missed the bag,"* *"she left too early,"* and *"it was right over!"*

Tie Score

Both teams have the same number of runs. One of many softball terms with roots in the garment world; for example, when the game is *tied*, the team's best *jock* might *collar* a ground ball with a *shoestring* catch and *snap* it to first to retire the side. Then she gets up and *belts* the game *capping* homer, *pants* for a minute, then rides off into the *vest* while the fans scream "*Raincoat!*" (Okay, that wasn't all real; she's probably in good enough shape that she never *pants*).

Tip

1. A foul ball that is barely touched by the bat, altering its path only slightly. In fast pitch, this change of direction typically causes the ball to miss the catcher's glove.
2. Fast pitch catchers—wear a cup.

Top of the Inning

The first part of an inning, when the visiting team bats. The bottom of the inning is the last part, when the home team bats, unless they last to the bottom of the last on top.

TOP O' THE INNING

Traction

1. The grip of spikes on the ground, which allows movement without slips and falls.
2. Hospital gear that prevents movement by players without spikes.

Trap

1. To appear to catch a ball in the air, while actually letting it bounce before catching it.
2. A facial orifice that is best kept shut when one realizes a teammate has trapped the ball.

Turf

The playing surface. Artificial turf is composed of a plastic, carpet-like material. Natural turf is composed of dirt, mud, sand, clay, clumps of weeds, stones, bottle caps, rusty nails, and broken glass.

Unbeaten

Looking forward to the first game of the season.

Umpire

An individual who determines the outcome of pitches and fielding plays, through solid knowledge of the rules, careful attention to the action on the field, and arbitrary guesswork.

Underhand

Delivery of a throw from the bottom of a downward circle. Other types include *overhand* (delivery from the top of an upward circle) and *offhand* (delivery from wherever).

Uniforms

Team garments that are all the same, i.e., left at home on game day.

Up

At the plate, batting. Also, really psyched to play well in a big game. Curiously, a player can be *up* for a big game, and, *up* at bat *in* a clutch situation, hit one *down* the line *right* at the *left* fielder for an *out*. What a *down*.

Veteran

An experienced player. While veterans may not be as fast or strong as a young player, they possess valuable knowledge gained from years of play, such as the location of the nearest bar, the location of the nearest bushes, and the location of the nearest hiding place when it comes time to carry the bases back to the rec department equipment shed.

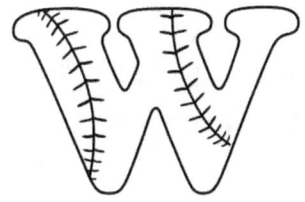

Walk

In a particularly sympathetic aspect of the softball rules, a batter who has four balls is allowed to walk to first base.

Warm Up

1. What a player never does before the game.
2. What the weather never does before the season.

WARM UP ROUTINE

WARM UPS
RUN 2 LAPS
STRETCH 2 MINS
TOSS 12 BALLS
TOSS BACK 12 OZ

Well-Oiled

Loose. A well-oiled team is relaxed and works together effectively. A well-oiled glove is flexible and easy to catch with. A well-oiled player is drunk and falls down a lot.

Wheelhouse

The strike zone. "Put it in the wheelhouse" is a catcher's colorful phrase for "throw a strike." This term derives from naval warfare, wherein a well-aimed shell would hit the enemy ship in the wheelhouse, causing the most damage. Other areas of endeavor have also contributed catcher's expressions for "throw a strike": plumbing (*down the pipe*), music (*groove it*), and cooking (*no batter*).

Whiff

A swinging strikeout. Derived from the sound made by the bat swishing through the air. A variation, used for swinging strikeouts in clutch situations, is *whiffuck*.

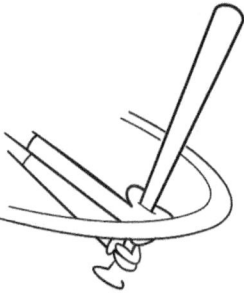

Wild

1. Unwilling to stop late-night partying, thus a pitcher is
2. Unable to get the ball over the plate.

Wind

1. Movement of air across the playing field. Can affect a player's throwing accuracy. Often present at softball games.
2. The ability of a player to exert his or herself continuously without exhaustion. Can affect a player's running speed. Rarely present at softball games.
3. Noisy movement of intestinal gasses out of a player's body. Can affect other players' ability to remain serious. Always present at the annual church "Bean Supper and Softball Game."

Wind Up

The arm motion of a pitcher just before delivering the pitch. Not to be confused with *drink up*, the arm motion of a pitcher just before going out to pitch.

XL

The shirt size worn by the thinnest softball players.

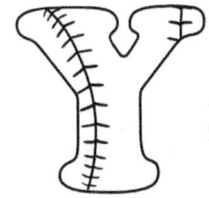

Yarn

1. Fuzzy, drawn-out material wound around a core of cork in softball manufacturing.
2. Fuzzy, drawn-out exaggerations wound around a core of truth in softball reminiscing.

Year

Measurement period of a team's success. Exact meaning depends on the modifier that precedes it, e.g., *bad* (this year) or *good* (next year).

Youth

Valuable characteristic of a player. Often comes with skill, athleticism, stamina, and sobriety.

Zero

A digit signifying "none." Typically represents your win total, the first digit of your batting average, and your chance of impressing your hot neighbor with the fact that you play rec-league softball.

Thank you!

Thanks for reading my humorous tribute to the game we love. I would appreciate it if you would post a review on Amazon.com or Goodreads.com. Writers depend on reviews to help others discover our books, so please share the fun. (If this was a gift, please thank the giver for me, then ask *them* to also post a review saying what a great gift it was!)

How to Succeed in Rec-League Softball

This book came about over many years of playing and managing softball with the Dawgs summer league team. Along the way, we discovered a few tips that, when occasionally followed, helped us play better without actually improving our skills. I've gathered those into a brief, light guide: *How to Succeed In Rec-League Softball*. You can get it, along with the simple score sheet we developed to replace hard-to-use scorebooks and unreliable scraps of paper.

Go to **daveagans.com** (or scan the QR code) and click on *Get The Softball Guide* to have a copy emailed to you and hear about future softball fun.

Dave Agans

Acknowledgments

Huge thanks to Manuel Sarmiento for rendering my cartoon concepts so hilariously; if you like his style and need artistic help, you can find him on Upwork.com. I can't say enough about the editorial and layout staff at B. Mirthy & Sons. And thanks to the many people who helped and encouraged me in producing this book, including my wife Gail and daughters Jen and Liz; my fellow writers at the New Hampshire Writers Project, the Nittany Valley Writers Network, Pennwriters, and Inkwell; and of course, several generations of Dawgs softball players, whose antics have entertained me for 350 dog years.

Dave Agans

www.ingramcontent.com/pod-product-compliance
Lightning Source LLC
Chambersburg PA
CBHW082245300426
44110CB00036B/2446